Spell-Write
An Aid to Spelling and Writing

Cedric Croft with Lia Mapa

NEW ZEALAND COUNCIL FOR EDUCATIONAL RESEARCH
TE RŪNANGA O AOTEAROA MŌ TE RANGAHAU I TE MĀTAURANGA

Wellington 1998

New Zealand Council for Educational Research
PO Box 3237 Wellington
New Zealand

© NZCER, 1998

ISBN 1–877140–33–3 (revised edition, 1998)

Reprinted 1999, 2000, 2001

Spell-Write was first published in 1983. ISBN 0–908567–30–8

Design: Peter Ridder and Robert McAlister

Distributed by NZCER Distribution Services
PO Box 3237, Wellington, New Zealand

Contents

About *Spell-Write (Revised)*	5
Using this Book to Help with Spelling and Writing	7
Learning to Spell a Word	8
Alphabetical List	9
Essential Words for Spelling and Writing	32
Groups of Words for Spelling and Writing	35
Commonly Misspelt Words	42
Hints on Spelling other Words	43

About *Spell-Write (Revised)*

This revised edition of *Spell-Write* replaces the original edition published in 1983 with 12 impressions up to 1997. The revision is based on research designed by the author of the original edition, Cedric Croft, Chief Research Officer NZCER, and administered by Lia Mapa, Research Assistant NZCER.

The research, which identified the approximately 3,400 words for this revision, included analyses of written scripts from 1,200 students from Years 3–8, attending a representative sample of 52 primary and intermediate schools in 1996–97.

For this revision, words no longer commonly used in primary school writing have been removed from the 'Alphabetical List' and new, more common words have been added. The sections 'Essential Words for Spelling and Writing' and 'Groups of Words for Spelling and Writing' have been extended and reorganised. Entries in the 'Commonly Misspelt Words' section have been reduced. The flow chart 'Learning to Spell a Word' has been retained with minor changes, but the section 'Place Names and Special Names', which was available for schools to complete, has been removed. A new section 'Hints on Spelling Other Words' has been added.

Spell-Write (Revised), and the research it is based on, reflect the important principle that spelling is primarily a skill of writing, which is best mastered within the context of learning to write. However, it needs to be acknowledged that writing by itself is unlikely to be sufficient for most children. There are important benefits for learning to spell from participating in a well-planned classroom programme of word study, built around the 'Essential Words' and 'Groups of Words' published in *Spell-Write (Revised)*.

Cedric Croft

Using this Book
to Help with Spelling and Writing

This book may be used to help with spelling *when you are writing*, or when you come to *proof-read your work*. There are also lists of the most common words you will write and groups of words on some topics. Your teacher will explain how to use the book in other ways.

1. If you are not sure how to spell a word, say the word carefully to yourself, and work out the letter it begins with.

2. Now find that letter in the alphabet down the side of this page. The number beside the letter tells you which page of the Alphabetical List to turn to.

3. Turn to the right page, and see if you can find the word.

4. This book does not have all the words you may need, but only the words written most often by New Zealand children. The meanings of some words are explained like this: their (their house); there (over there).

Personal Spelling Lists

1. If you have a *Personal Spelling List*, your teacher will want you to enter some words from *Spell-Write*, in your list.

2. You should learn all the words in your *Personal Spelling List*, so you can use them in your own writing. One way to learn new words is set out on page 8 of this book.

	Page
A	9
B	10
C	11
D	13
E	14
F	15
G	16
H	17
I	18
J	18
K	19
L	19
M	20
N	21
O	22
P	22
Q	24
R	24
S	25
T	28
U	29
V	30
W	30
X	31
Y	31
Z	31

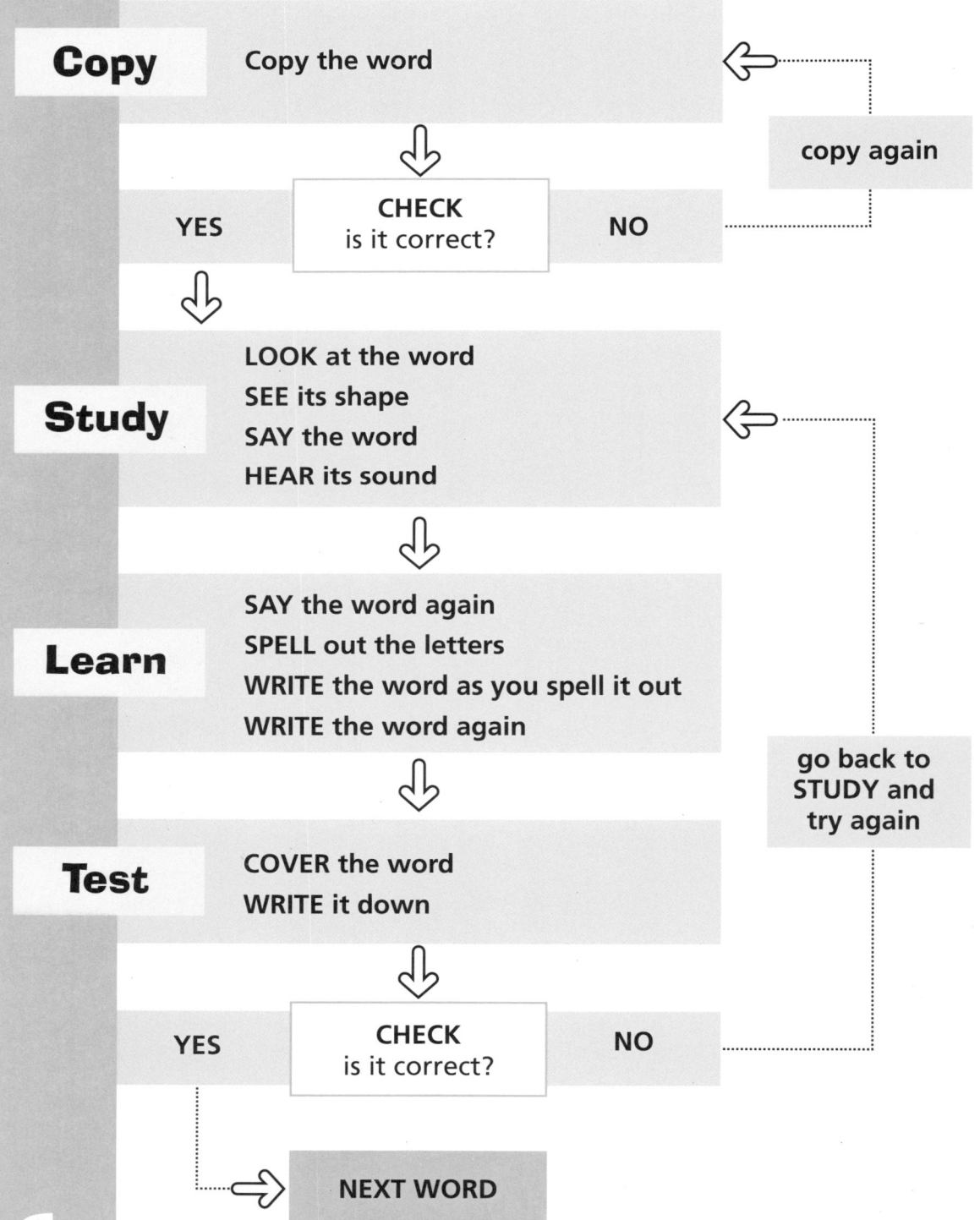

Alphabetical List

This section contains many words you will use in your writing. Use this list when you want to find out how to spell a particular word.
If you have a *Personal Spelling List,* your teacher will explain which of these words should be written in it.

abandon
ability
able
aboard
about
above
absence
absent
absolutely
accident
accidentally
account
ache
achieve
across
act
action
active
activities
activity
actual
actually
add
addition
address
admit
adopted
adult
advantage
adventure
advice
aeroplane
afford
afraid
after
afternoon
afterwards
again
against
age
ago
agree
agreement
agriculture
ahead
aid
aim
aimed
air
aircraft
airline
airport
alarm
alert
alien
alike
alive
all
alleyway
alligator
allow
allowed (may go)
all right
almost
alone
along
aloud (read aloud)
already
also
although
altogether
always
am
amaze
amazing
ambulance
among
amount
amuse
an
ancestor
ancient
and
angel (be an angel)
anger
angle (a sharp turn)
angry
animal
ankle
announce
annoy
another
answer
answered
ant
anxious
any
anybody
anyhow
any more
anyone
anything
anyway
anywhere
apart
apologise
appear
appearance
appeared
apple
appreciation
approach
April
apron
arcade
are
area

aren't

aren't (are not)
argue
arguing
argument
arm
army
around
arrange
arrest
arrested
arrival
arrive
arrived
arriving
arrow
art
article
artist
as
ashamed
ashes
ashore
aside
ask
asked
asleep
assembly
association
at
ate (ate lunch)
atmosphere
atom
atomic
attack
attend
attention
attic
attract
attractive

audience
August
aunt (Aunt Jill)
auntie
aunty
author
automatic
autumn
avenue
average
awake
away
awesome
awful
awhile
awoke
axe

babies
baby
baby-sitter
back
backwards
backyard
bacon
bad
badge
badly
bag
bait
bake
bakery
baking
balance
ball
ballet

balloon
banana
band
bang
bank
bar
barbecue
bare (uncovered)
bark
barn
barrel
barrier
base
baseball
basket
basketball
bat
batch
bath
bathe
bathroom
battery
battle
bay
be (be happy)
beach
bead
beam
bean (vegetable)
bear (animal)
beast
beat
beaten
beautiful
beauty
became
because
become
bed

bike

bedroom
bee (honey bee)
beef
been (I have been)
beer
beetle
before
beg
began
begin
beginning
begun
behave
behaviour
behind
being
believe
bell
belong
belongings
below
belt
bench
bend
beneath
bent
berries
berry (fruit)
beside
best
bet
better
between
bible
bicycle (bike)
big
bigger
biggest
bike (bicycle)

bill

cap

bill
billion
billionaire
bird
birth
birthday
biscuit
bit
bite
black
blade
blanket
blast
bleed
blew
　(the wind blew)
blind
blink
block
blood
blossom
blow
blown
blue (colour)
board
　(piece of wood)
boat
bodies
body
boil
bomb
bone
bonfire
book
booklet
boom
boot
border
bored (not interested)

boring
born
borrow
boss
bossy
both
bother
bottle
bottom
bought (buy)
boulder
bounce
bound
boundary
bow
bowl
box
boxes
boy
boyfriend
brain
brake (car brake)
branch
branches
brass
brave
bread (bread to eat)
break (damage)
breakfast
breast
breath
breathe
breathing
breeze
brick
bridge
bright
brightly
bring

broadcast
broke
broken
bronze
broom
brother
brought (bring)
brown
brownie
bruise
brush
bubble
bucket
bud
buddy
build
built
bulb
bull
bulldozer
bullet
bump
bunch
bundle
burglar
buried
burn
burnt
burrow
burst
bury (bury rubbish)
bus
buses
bush
bushes
business
busy
but
butcher

butter
butterfly
button
buy (buy the milk)
by (by the sea)
bye (good bye)

Cc

cabbage
cabin
cabinet
cafe
cage
cake
calendar
calf
call
called
calm
calves
came
camel
camera
camp
can
canary
cancer
candle
candy
cane
cannibal
cannon
cannot (can't)
canoe
can't (cannot)
canvas
cap

capital   competition

capital
capsule
captain
capture
car
caravan
card
cardboard
care
careful
carefully
careless
caring
carpenter
carpet
carriage
carried
carries
carrot
carry
carrying
cart
case
cassette
cast
castle
cat
catch
catches
cattle
caught (to catch)
cause
cave
ceiling (inside roof)
celebrate
celebration
celery (vegetable)
cellar
cement

cemetery
centimetre
central
centre
cents
centuries
century
certain
chain
chair
chalk
championship
chance
change
changing
chapter
character
charge
chart
chase
chasing
cheap (low cost)
check (check up)
cheek (face)
cheer
cheerful
cheese
chemist
cheque (money)
cherry
chest
chew (eat)
chicken
chief
child
children
chimney
chip
chocolate

choice
choir
choose (pick)
choosing
chop
chopped
chopping
chorus
chose (picked)
chosen
Christmas
church
churches
circle
circuit
circus
cities
citizen
city
civil
clapped
class
classes
classroom
claws
clay
clean
clear
clever
click
cliff
climate
climb
climbed
clinic
cloak
clock
close
closing

cloth
clothes
clothing
cloud
clown
club
clue
coach
coal
coast
coat
cobweb
cocoa
coconut
coffee
coffin
cold
collar
collect
collection
college
colour
coloured
colourful
colt
comb
come
comfortable
comic
coming
command
commercial
committee
common
community
companion
company
compass
competition

competitor   delicious

competitor
complain
complete
completely
computer
concerned
concert
concrete
condition
cone
confidence
connect
consider
contact
contain
container
content
contest
continent
continue
control
conversation
cook
cooked
cool
copper
copy
corn
corner
correct
corridor
cost
costume
cosy
cottage
cotton
couch
cough
could

couldn't (could not)
council
count
counter
countries
country
couple
courage
course (path; subject)
court
   (tennis/law court)
cousin
cover
covered
cow
cowboy
crab
crack
crackers
craft
crane
crash
crashed
crashes
crawl
crayfish
crazy
creak (noise)
cream
created
creature
creek (stream)
creep
crept
crew
cricket
cried
cries
crime

criminal
cripple
crisp
crocodile
crop
cross
crowd
crown
cruel
crumb
crush
crust
cry
crying
cub
cuddle
cup
cupboard
cure
curiosity
curious
curly
current
curtain
curve
cushion
customer
cut
cute
cutting
cycle

Dd

dad
daddy
daily
dairy (shop)

daisies
daisy
dam
damage
damp
dance
dancing
danger
dangerous
dare
dark
darkness
dart
dash
data
date
daughter
dawn
day
daylight
dead
deaf
deal
dear
   (loved; expensive)
death
December
decent
decide
decided
decision
deck
decorate
deed
deep
deer (animal)
definitely
degree
delicious

delight

delight
delighted
deliver
dense
dental
dentist
describe
description
desert (sandy place; abandon)
design
desk
dessert (pudding)
destination
destroy
detention
determined
develop
development
devil
dew (damp)
dial
diamond
diaries
diary (write a diary)
dictionaries
dictionary
did
didn't (did not)
die (death; dying)
died
difference
different
difficult
dig
digest
digging
dinghy (small boat)

dingy (dull)
dining
dinner
dinosaur
dip
direction
dirt
dirty
disagree
disappear
disappeared
disappoint
disaster
disco
discover
disease
dish
dishes
display
distance
distant
district
disturb
ditch
dive
divide
diving
division
do
doctor
dodge
does
doesn't (does not)
dog
doing
doll
dollars
dolphin
done

donkey
don't (do not)
door
double
down
downstairs
dozen
dragon
drank
draw (draw a line)
drawer (desk drawer)
drawn
dream
drenched
dress
dressed
dresses
drew
dried
drill
drink
drip
drive
driveway
driving
drop
dropped
drove
drown
drug
drum
drunk
dry
duck
due (the bus is due)
dug
dull
dumb

eighth

dump
dungeon
dunk
during
dust
duty
dwarf
dwarves
dye (colour)
dying (death; die)

each
eagle
ear
earlier
early
earn
earphones
earth
earthquake
easier
easily
east
Easter
eastern
easy
eat
eaten
edge
editor
eel
effort
egg
eight (number 8)
eighteen
eighth

eighty   **finally**

eighty · essay · explore · fat
either · eve · explosion · father
elbow · even · express · fault
elect · evening · extra · favour
election · event · extremely · favourite
electric · eventually · eye · fear (be afraid)
electricity · ever · · feast
electronic · every · · feather
elephant · everybody · · February
eleven · everyday (each day) · · fed
elf · every day (usual) · · feed

else · everyone · face · feel
elves · everything · fact · feeling
embarrass · everywhere · factory · feet
emergency · evil · fade · fell
empty · ewe (female sheep) · fail · fellow
encyclopedia · exactly · faint · felt
end · exam · fainted · female
enemy · examination · fair (gala; correct) · fence
energy · example · fairies · fern
engine · excellent · fairly · ferocious
engineer · except · fairy (fairy tale) · ferry (ship)
English · exchange · faithful · fertile
enjoy · excited · fake · fetch
enjoyable · excitement · fall · fever
enjoyed · exciting · fallen · few
enormous · excuse · false · field
enough · exercise · familiar · fierce
enter · exhausted · families · fifteen
entered · exhibit · family · fifth
entertain · exhibition · famous · fifty
entirely · expect · fan · fight
entrance · expedition · fancy · figure
envelope · expense · fantastic · fill
equal · expensive · far · filled
equipment · experience · farm · film
eraser (rubber) · experiment · fascinated · filthy
escape · explain · fast · final
especially · explode · fasten · finally
· · fastest ·

find   **ginger**

find
fine
finger
finish
finished
fire
fireman
fireplace
fireworks
first
fish
fisherman
fist
fit
fitted
five
fix
flag
flame
flannel
flap
flapping
flare
flash
flat
flavour
flax
fled
flesh
flew
flies
flight
float
flock
flood
floor
flour
  (used for baking)
flow

flower (plant)
fluffy
fly
flying
foal
foggy
fold
folk
follow
followed
food
fool
foolish
foot
football
footpath
footsteps
for
force
forced
forecast
forehead
foreign
forest
forever
forget
forgetful
forgive
forgot
forgotten
fork
form
formula
fort (building)
fortunate
fortune
forty
forward
fought (wrestled)

found
fountain
four (number 4)
fourteen
fourth
fox
frame
freckles
free
freedom
freeze
freezing
freight
fresh
Friday
fridge (refrigerator)
fried
friend
friendly
friends
friendship
fright
frighten
frightened
frog
from
front
frost
froze
frozen
fruit
fuel
full
fun
funeral
funny
fur (animal's skin)
furious
furnish

furniture
furry
further
future

G g

gain
gala
gale
gallop
game
gang
garage
garden
garlic
gas
gasp
gate
gather
gave
gay
gaze
gear
geese
general
gentle
gentleman
geography
germ
get
getting
ghost
giant
gift
gigantic
giggle
ginger

giraffe

giraffe
girl
girlfriend
give
given
giving
glacier
glad
glass
glasses
glitter
glove
glue
go
goal
goat
go-cart
God
goes
going
gold
golden
goldfish
golf
gone
good
goodbye
goodness
goodnight
goose
gorilla (animal)
got
government
grab
grabbed
graceful
grade
gradually
grain

gram
grand
granddad
grandfather
grandma
grandmother
grandpa
grandparents
granny
granted
grapes
grass
grateful
grave
gravel
graveyard
graze
grazing
grease
great
greedy
green
grew
grey
grill
groan (cry of pain)
groceries
ground
group
grow
growl
grown (grown taller)
growth
guard
guess
guest
guide
guinea pig
gum

gumboots
gun
guy
gymnastics

habit
had
hadn't (had not)
hail
hair (hair style)
hairy
half
halfway
hall (meeting place)
hallway
halves
ham
hamburger
hammer
hand
handful
handkerchief
handle
handy
hang
hangi
   (meal; earth oven)
happen
happened
happily
happiness
happy
harbour
hard
harden
hardly

he'll

hare (animal)
harm
harvest
has
hasn't (has not)
hat
hatch
hate
haul (pull along)
haunt
haunted
have
haven't (have not)
having
hawk
hay (dried grass)
he
head
headmaster
heal (get better)
health
healthy
heap
hear (listen)
heard (listened)
heart
heat
heater
heaven
heavier
heavy
he'd (he would)
hedge
hedgehog
heel (part of foot)
height
held
helicopter
he'll (he will)

hello   jail

hello	hook		ink
helmet	hooves		innocent
help	hop		insect
helpful	hope	I (me)	inside
hen	hoping	ice	inspect
her	hopped	iceberg	instance
herd (herd of cattle)	hopping	iceblock	instead
here (here and there)	horizontal	icecream	instrument
hero	horn	icy	intelligent
herself	horrible	I'd (I would)	interest
hey (call out)	horror	idea	interested
hid	horse	idle	interesting
hidden	hose	if	intermediate
hide	hospital	I'll (I will)	interval
hiding	hostage	ill	into
high	hot	illness	invent
highway	hot dog	I'm (I am)	invention
hike	hotel	imaginary	investigate
hill	hour (60 minutes)	imagination	invisible
him	house	imagine	invitation
himself	household	immediately	invite
his	how	importance	invited
history	however	important	iron
hit	hug	impossible	irrigation
hitting	huge	improve	is
hobbies	hugged	in	island
hobby	human	inch	isn't (is not)
hockey	hundred	including	it
hold	hung	increase	item
hole (dig a hole)	hungry	indeed	it's (it is)
holiday	hunt	independence	its (its tail)
hollow	hunting	independent	itself
holy (sacred)	hurricane	index	I've (I have)
home	hurried	indoors	
homework	hurries	industry	
honest	hurry	information	
honey	hurt	injured	
honour	husband	injuries	jacket
hoof	hut	injury	jail

I i

J j

jam   **life**

jam		knock	lay
jandals		knocked	lazy
January		knot (tie a knot)	lead (to lead; metal)
jar	kangaroo	knotted	leader
jaw	kauri (kauri tree)	know (I know)	leaf
jealous	keen	knowledge	league
jeans	keep	known	leak (drip)
jeep	kennel	koala	leap
jellies	kept	kumara (vegetable)	learn
jelly	kettle		learnt
jersey	key		least
jet	kick		leather
jewel	kicked		leave
jewellery	kid		leaves
jingle	kill	labour	leaving
job	killed	lace	led (led the race)
join	kilogram	lack	left
joke	kilometre	ladder	leg
jolly	kind	ladies	legend
journal	kindergarten	lady	leisure
journey	kindness	laid	lemon
joy	king	lake	lemonade
judge	kingdom	lamb	lend
judging	kiss	lame	length
juice	kit	lamp	lent
juicy	kitchen	land	less
July	kite	landed	lesson
jump	kitten	language	let
jumped	kiwi	lantern	let's (let us)
June	knee	lap	letter
jungle	kneel	large	letting
junior	knelt	laser	lettuce
junk	knew (we knew)	last	level
just	knife	late	library
justice	knight (warrior)	later	licence (TV licence)
	knit	laugh	lick
	knitting	laughed	lid
	knives	law	lie
	knob	lawn	life
		lawyer	

lift — mighty

lift
light
lightning
  (flash of light)
like
liking
limb
lime
limit
limousine
limp
line
linen
lion
lipstick
liquid
list
listen
lit
litre
little
live
lived
lives
living
lizard
load
loaded
loaf
loaves
lock
locked
log
lollies
lolly
lonely
long
look
looked

looking
loose (not tight)
lorry
lose (can't find)
lost
lot
lots
loud
loudly
lounge
love
lovely
loving
low
luck
luckily
lucky
luggage
lump
lunch
lunch time
lung
lying

Mm

machine
machinery
mad
made
magazine
magic
magical
magnet
magnetic
magnificent
maid (girl)
mail (letter)

main
mainly
majority
make
making
male (boy or man)
mall
mammal
man
manage
manager
manner
manufacture
manufacturing
manuka
  (manuka tree)
many
Maori
map
marae
  (meeting place)
marble
March
mare (female horse)
mark
market
married
marry
marvellous
mask
mass
massive
mast
master
mat
match
matches
mate
material

mathematics
maths
matter
May
maybe (perhaps)
may be
  (it may be true)
mayor (city leader)
me
meal
mean
meant
meanwhile
measles
measure
meat
  (from a butcher)
medal
medicine
meet (meet me)
melt
member
memories
memory
men
merry
mess
message
met
metal
meter
  (parking meter)
method
metre (distance; 1m)
mice
middle
midnight
might
mighty

mile

mile
military
milk
millilitre
millimetre
million
millionaire
mind (look after)
mine
mineral
minister
minute
   (60 seconds; tiny)
mirror
mischief
miserable
miss
missed (missed out)
missile
mission
mist (low cloud)
mistake
misty
mix
moan
model
modelling
modern
moisture
moment
Monday
money
monkey
monster
month
moon
more (extra)
morning
   (before midday)

moss
most
mostly
motel
moth
mother
motion
motive
motor
motorbike
mould
mount
mountain
mountainous
mouse
mouth
move
movement
movies
moving
mow
mower
Mr
Mrs
Ms
much
mud
muddy
multiply
mum
mummy
mumps
murder
muscles (leg or arm)
museum
music
musical
mussels (shellfish)
must

my
myself
mysteries
mysterious
mystery

nail
name
nana (grandmother)
narrow
nasty
nation
national
native
natural
naturally
nature
naughty
navy
near
nearby
nearest
nearly
neat
necessary
neck
necklace
need
needle
neighbour
neighbourhood
neither
nephew
nervous
nest
net

nowhere

netball
netting
never
new (new car)
news
newspaper
next
nice
niece
night (darkness)
nightmare
nine
nineteen
ninety
ninth
no
nobody
nodded
noise (sound)
noisy
none
noon
no one
nor
   (neither you nor he)
normal
normally
north
northern
nose (your nose)
not (not going)
note
notebook
nothing
notice
noticing
November
now
nowhere

nuclear

nuclear
nuisance
numb
number
nurse
nut
nylon

oak (tree)
oasis
oats
obey
object
obtain
obviously
occasion
occasionally
occupation
occupied
occupy
occur
ocean
o'clock
October
octopus
odd
of (piece of cake)
off (fell off)
offer
office
officer
often
oh (oh my!)
oil
okay (OK)
old

older
on
once
one (number 1)
onion
only
on to
open
opened
opera
operate
operating
operation
opportunity
opposite
or (this or that)
orange
orchard
orchestra
order
ordinary
organ
organise
other
otherwise
ouch
ought
our (our house)
ourselves
out
outdoors
outline
outside
oven
over
overalls
overhead
overseas
owe (owe money)

owing
owl
own
owner
oxygen
oyster

Pp

pa (Maori village)
pack
packed
packet
pad
paddle
paddock
page
paid
pain (soreness)
paint
painted
pair (pair of shoes)
palace
pale (light in colour)
palm
pan
panel
panic
pants
paper
parachute
parade
paragraph
parcel
pardon
parents
park
parked

perfume

parliament
parrot
part
particular
parties
partner
party
pass
passage
passed
  (he passed me)
passenger
past (in the past)
paste
pat
patch
path
patrol
patted
pattern
paw (animal's foot)
pay
payment
peace
  (peace not war)
peaceful
peach
peak
peanut
pear (fruit)
peas
pen
pencil
penguin
people
pepper
perfect
perfectly
perfume

## perhaps																								pump

perhaps	planet	pool	prettier
period	planned	poor (needy)	prettiest
permission	planning	pop	pretty
person	plant	popular	prevent
pet	plantation	population	price
petrol	plastic	porch	primary
phone (telephone)	plate	porridge	prince
photo	platform	port	princess
photograph	play	position	principal (chief)
phrase	playcentre	possible	principle (idea)
piano	played	possibly	print
pick	playful	post	prison
picked	playground	postage	private
picnic	playing	poster	prize
picture	playtime	postman	probably
pie	pleasant	pot	problem
piece (piece of pie)	please	potato	process
pig	pleasure	potatoes	produce
pigeon	plenty	pounce	product
pile	plough	pound	production
pill	plus	pour (pour milk)	professor
pillow	pocket	powder	program
pilot	poem	power	(computer program)
pin	poet	powerful	programme
pinch	poetry	practice	progress
pine	point	(singing practice)	project
pink	poison	practise	promise
pioneer	polar	(to practise singing)	proper
pipe	pole	practising	property
pipi (shellfish)	police	pray	protect
pirate	policeman	prayer	protection
pit	policewoman	precious	proud
pitch	polished	preparation	prove
pity	polite	prepare	provide
pizza	political	present	public
place	pollution	president	pudding
plain (simple; flat land)	pond	press	pull
plan	ponies	pressure	pulled
plane (aeroplane; tool)	pony	pretend	pump

23

pumpkin

pumpkin
punch
puncture
punish
pup
pupil
puppet
puppies
puppy
pure
purple
purpose
purse
push
pushed
put
putting
puzzle
pyjamas

quality
quantity
quarrel
quarter
queen
queer
question
queue (line up)
quick
quickly
quiet (silent)
quietly
quite (quite right)

rabbit
race
races
racing
radar
radio
raffle
raft
rag
ragged
rail
railway
rain
rainbow
raincoat
raining
rainy
raise
raised
raising
rake
ran
rang
range
rapidly
rare
rat
rather
raw (not cooked)
reach
reached
read (read a book)
ready
real
realise
really

reason
receive
recent
recipe
recognise
record
recreation
rectangle
red (colour)
reef
referee
refreshments
refuse
regard
region
regular
relation
relative
relax
relay
release
relief
religion
religious
remain
remember
remembered
remind
rent
repeat
replied
reply
report
reptile
rescue
reserve
resist
respect
rest

rotten

restaurant
result
return
returned
reward
ribbon
rice
rich
ride
riding
rifle
right
   (correct; right hand)
ring
ripe
ripped
rise
river
road (street)
roam
roar (loud noise)
roast
rob
robbed
robber
robot
rock
rocket
rod
rode (rode a bike)
roll
roof
room
rooster
root (plant)
rope
rose
rot
rotten

rough   **shiver**

rough
round
route (path, course)
row
rub
rubbed
rubber
rubbish
rubble
rug
rugby
ruin
rule
run
runner
running
rush
rushed
rusty

Ss

sack
sad
saddle
sadly
safe
safely
safety
said
sail (boat)
sailor
salad
sale (shop)
salmon
salt
salute
same

sand
sandals
sandwich
sandy
sang
sank
sat
satisfied
satisfy
Saturday
sauce (tomato sauce)
saucepan
saucer
sauna
sausage
save
saving
saw
    (tool; saw the parade)
say
scale
scarce
scare
scared (afraid)
scarf
scaring
scary
scene (view)
scenery
school
science
scientist
scissors
score
scout
scramble
scrap
scratch
scream

screamed
screen
screw
scribble
scrub
scrubbing
sea (ocean)
seagull
seal
seam (sew a seam)
search
seaside
season
seat
second
secret
secretary
section
see (see this)
seed
seek
seem (seem to)
seemed
seen (I have seen)
seldom
self
sell
send
senior
sense
sensible
sent (sent a card)
sentence
separate
September
serious
servant
serve
service

set
setting
settle
settler
seven
seventeen
seventh
seventy
several
sew (sew clothes)
shade
shadow
shady
shake
shaking
shall
shape
share
shark
sharp
she
shearing
shed
sheep
sheet
shelf
shell
shellfish
shelter
shelves
she's (she is)
shield
shift
shine
shining
shiny
ship
shirt
shiver

shock   **space**

shock	similar	slice	snowman
shoe	simple	slid	so (so small)
shone	since	slide	soak
shook	sincerely	sliding	soaked
shoot	sing	slim	soap
shop	single	slime	soccer
shopkeeper	sink	slimy	social
shopping	sir	slip	socks
shore	siren	slipped	sofa
short	sister	slippers	soft
shorts	sit	slippery	softball
shot	sitting	slow	softly
should	situated	slowly	soil
shoulder	situation	smack	solar
shouldn't	six	small	sold
(should not)	sixteen	smallest	soldier
shout	sixth	smart	solid
shouted	sixty	smash	solo
shovel	size	smashed	solution
show	skate	smell	solve
showed	skateboard	smelly	some (some girls)
shower	skating	smelt	somebody
shown	skeleton	smile	somehow
shriek	ski	smiling	someone
shut	skiing	smoke	something
sick	skin	smoking	sometimes
sickness	skinny	smooth	somewhere
side	skip	snake	son (boy)
sideways	skipping	snap	song
sigh	skirt	snapped	soon
sight (eyesight)	skull	snatched	sore (painful)
sign	sky	sneak	sorry
signal	slam	sneaked	sort
signalled	slammed	sneezed	sound
silence	slave	sniff	soup
silent	sleep	snores	sour
silk	sleeping	snoring	south
silly	sleepy	snow	southern
silver	slept	snowball	space

spacecraft   sunny

spacecraft
spaceship
spade
spare (spare tyre)
sparkle
speak
spear (weapon)
special
spectators
speech
speed
spell
spend
spent
spice
spider
spill
spilt
spin
spinning
spirit
splash
splendid
split
spoil
spoke
spoon
sport
spot
spotted
sprain
sprang
spread
spring
spun
spy
square
squash
squeak

squeeze
squid
squirt
stab
stabbed
stable
stack
stadium
stag
stage
stain
stairs (steps)
stall
stallion
stamp
stand
standard
standing
star
stare (look at)
staring
start
started
starve
starving
state
statement
station
stationary
 (not moving)
stationery (paper)
statue
stay
stayed
staying
steady
steak (meat)
steal (rob)
steam

steel (metal)
steep
steer
stem
step
stepped
stereo
stew
stick
sticky
stiff
still
sting
stir
stitch
stock
stole
stolen
stomach
stone
stood
stool
stop
stopped
stopping
store
storey
 (level of building)
storeys
stories (tales)
storm
stormy
story (tale)
stove
straight
 (straight line)
stranded
strange
strap

straw
stray
stream
street
strength
stretch
strike
string
strip
strong
struck
struggle
stuck
student
study
stuff
stumble
stupid
subject
submarine
subtract
succeed
success
successful
such
sudden
suddenly
sugar
suggest
suit
suitable
suitcase
sum (maths; total)
summer
sun (hot sun)
sunbathe
Sunday
sung
sunny

sunrise

sunrise
sunset
sunshine
super
supermarket
supper
supplies
supply
support
suppose
supposing
sure
surely
surf
surface
surprise
surprised
surprising
surrender
surround
survive
suspicious
swallow
swam
swamp
sway
sweat
sweep
sweet
swell
swept
swift
swim
swimming
swing
switch
sword
swum
swung
system

Tt

table
tadpole
tag
tail (dog's tail)
take
taken
taking
tale (story)
talk
talked
tall
tame
tan
tank
tap
tape
tar
target
taste
taught
tax
taxi
tea
teach
teacher
team
teapot
tear
tease
teaspoon
teeth
telephone
telescope
television (TV)
tell
temper

temperature
ten
tender
tennis
tent
tenth
term
terrible
terrific
terrified
terrify
test
than
thank
thankful
thank you
that
that's (that is)
the
theatre
theft
their (their house)
them
themselves
then
there (over there)
these
they
they're (they are)
thick
thief
thieves
thin
thing
things
think
third
thirsty
thirteen

tiny

thirty
this
thorn
those
though
thought
thoughtful
thousand
thread
three
threw (threw a ball)
thrifty
thrilled
throat
throne
through
  (through the door)
throughout
throw
thrown
thud
thumb
thump
thunder
Thursday
tick
ticket
tide (low tide)
tidied
tidy
tie
tied (tied a knot)
tiger
tight
till
timber
time
tin
tiny

tip   **useful**

tip	towel	trousers	unconscious
tiptoe	tower	trout	under
tired	town	truck	underground
title	toy	true	underneath
to (go to bed)	track	truly	understand
toast	tractor	trunk	understood
tobacco	trade	trust	underwater
today	traffic	truth	underwear
toe (part of foot)	tragedy	try	undo
toffee	trail	trying	undone
together	trailer	T-shirt	undressed
togs	train	tube	unfortunate
toilet	training	Tuesday	unfortunately
told	tramp	tumbled	unhappy
tomato	trampoline	tune	unidentified
tomatoes	transport	tunnel	uniform
tomorrow	trap	turkey	union
tongue	trapped	turn	unit
tonight	travel	turned	unite
too (too small)	travelled	TV (television)	united
took	traveller	twelfth	universe
tools	travelling	twelve	university
tooth	tray	twenty	unknown
toothbrush	treasure	twice	unless
toothpaste	treat	twig	unlucky
top	tree	twin	unpack
torch	trees	twins	untie
tore	tremble	two (number 2)	untied
torn	tremendous	type	until
toss	triangle	typewriter	unusual
total	tribe	tyre	up
totally	trick		upon
touch	tried	**U u**	upper
touched	tries		upset
tough	trigger		upstairs
tour	trimmed	ugly	us
tournament	trip	umbrella	use
tow (tow a car)	tripped	umpire	used
towards	trouble	uncle	useful

using

using
usual
usually

 **V** v

vacant
vacuum
valley
valuable
value
van
vanish
variety
various
varnish
vase
vegetables
vehicle
verse
very
vet (veterinarian)
video
view
village
vine
vinegar
violent
violet
violin
visible
visit
visitor
voice
volcano
vote
voyage

 **W** w

wag
wagged
wagon
waist
   (measure your waist)
wait (wait here)
waited
waiting
wake
walk
walked
walking
wall
wander
wandered
want
wanted
war (fighting)
wardrobe
warm
warmth
warn (alert)
warrior
was
wash
wasn't (was not)
wasp
waste (waste time)
watch
watched
water
waterfall
wave
way (direction)
we
weak (not strong)

wire

wealth
weapon
wear (wear a coat)
weather
   (wet weather)
weave
web
we'd (we would)
wedding
Wednesday
week (7 days)
weekend
weekly
weigh
   (weigh on scales)
weight (heavy)
weird
welcome
we'll (we will)
well
went
we're (we are)
were (we were here)
weren't (were not)
west
western
wet
we've (we have)
whale
wharf
wharves
what
whatever
what's (what is)
wheat
wheel
wheelbarrow
when
whenever

where
   (where are you?)
where's (where is)
wherever
whether
   (whether to)
which (which one?)
while
whip
whisper
whistle
white
whitebait
who
whoever
whole (total)
who's (who is)
whose (whose coat?)
why
wicked
wide
widow
width
wife
wild
will
win
wind
winding
windmill
window
windy
wine
wing
winner
winning
winter
wipe
wire

wise   **zoo**

wise	woollen	wrestling	yellow
wish	word	wriggle	yes
wished	wore (wore jeans)	wrist	yesterday
wishes	work	write (write a note)	yet
witch (the old witch)	world	writing	you (person)
witches	worm	written	you'll (you will)
with	worn (used)	wrong	young
within	worried	wrote	youngest
without	worry		your (your pet)
wives	worse		you're (you are)
wizard	worst		yourself
woke	worth		youth
wolf	would		you've (you have)
wolves	(would you go?)	X-ray	
woman	wouldn't		
women	(would not)		
won (won the match)	wound		
wonder	wrap (wrap the	yacht	zebra
wonderful	parcel)	yard	zero
won't (will not)	wrapped	yawn	zone
wood (timber)	wreath	year	zoo
wooden	wreck	yell	
wool	wrestle	yelled	

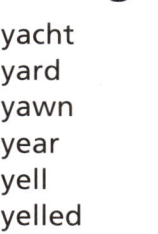

Essential Words
for Spelling and Writing

The 290 words in this section are used most often when you write. Together, they make up about three-quarters of most writing, so they are important.
These words have been arranged in alphabetical order and put in 7 lists according to how often they are used. The words in List 1 are used most often, the words in List 2 next most often, and so on. Because they are used so often, it is very important that you learn to use and spell each one.

Essential List 1 (10 Words; 25% of Writing)

a	I	it	the	was
and	in	my	to	we

Essential List 2 (20 Words; 15% of Writing)

at	had	of	that	up
but	he	on	then	went
for	is	she	there	when
got	me	so	they	you

Essential List 3 (30 Words; 10% of Writing)

about	be	go	into	our
after	because	going	just	out
all	came	have	like	said
are	day	her	mum	some
as	down	his	not	were
back	get	home	one	with

Essential List 4 (50 Words; 10% of Writing)

again	do	next	people	time
an	first	night	put	took
around	food	no	ran	two
big	from	now	saw	us
by	good	off	school	very
can	has	old	see	well
come	him	only	started	what
could	house	or	their	will
dad	if	other	them	would
did	little	over	this	your

Essential List 5 (50 Words; 5% of Writing)

am	door	last	once	through
another	everyone	left	play	told
away	family	long	really	too
bed	five	looked	room	walked
been	found	made	something	want
before	friend	man	still	way
best	fun	more	thing	where
brother	heard	morning	think	which
called	here	name	thought	who
car	know	never	three	year

Essential List 6 (70 Words; 5% of Writing)

also	cool	eyes	head	jump
always	dark	fell	hit	knew
asked	decided	felt	how	later
black	dog	find	inside	life
boy	eat	four	its	live
bus	end	gave	it's	lot
cat	even	getting	I'll	lunch
coming	every	great	I'm	make

minutes	place	sister	top	water
most	ready	sleep	town	while
much	ride	suddenly	tree	why
nice	right	take	turned	window
opened	run	tell	until	woke
outside	say	ten	wanted	yes

Essential List 7 (60 Words; 3% of Writing)

any	each	ground	money	soon
baby	ever	guard	mother	stay
bad	everything	hand	myself	stop
ball	face	happened	new	swimming
being	fast	happy	parents	tea
bit	father	help	picked	than
boat	few	hole	playing	tried
bought	finally	hot	presents	under
camp	finished	hour	road	wait
dead	game	let	side	won
died	girl	look	small	work
doing	gone	many	sometimes	world

Groups of Words
for Spelling and Writing

The words in this section, together with the *Essential Words for Spelling and Writing,* are among the most common words you will write. Here you will find groups of words about:

Numbers
One to nineteen
Twenty to ninety
Hundred and over

Time
Days
Months
Other days
Seasons
Units of time
When?

Amounts
How big?
How far?
How fast?
How much?
How old?
How valuable?
What kind?

Location
Buildings
Parts of building
Places
Where?

Nature
Animals
Body parts
Colours
Matter
Places
Plants
Sounds
Space
Water
Weather

Common Objects
Containers
Clothes
Food
House contents
Materials

People
Family
Others

Activities
Daily events
Feelings
Fighting
Games
Leisure
Movements
Not moving
Other actions
School
Talking
Thinking
Transport

Descriptions
Pleasant
Unpleasant
Unusual

The words in each group may help with your writing. For example, if you are writing about life in the country, you may find a group like 'Nature' helpful. Your teacher will tell you about other ways to use the lists and how to study the words.

Numbers

1. One to nineteen

one
two
three
four
five
six
seven
eight
nine
ten
eleven
twelve
thirteen
fourteen
fifteen
sixteen
seventeen
eighteen
nineteen

2. Twenty to ninety

twenty
thirty
forty
fifty
sixty
seventy
eighty
ninety

3. Hundred and over

hundred
thousand
million
billion

Time

1. Days

Sunday
Monday
Tuesday
Wednesday
Thursday
Friday
Saturday

2. Months

January
February
March
April
May
June
July
August
September
October
November
December

3. Other days

birthday
Christmas
everyday
holiday
today
tomorrow
weekend
yesterday

4. Seasons

spring
summer
autumn
winter

5. Units of time

moment
second
minute
hour
day
week
month
year

6. When?

afternoon
ago
already
during
early
finally
late
lunch time
morning
o'clock
past
ready
since
till
usually
yet

Amounts

1. How big?

big
fat
giant
great
huge
large
tall

2. How far?
closer
distance
far
near

3. How fast?
quickly
slowly
suddenly

4. How many?
both
couple
double
group
lot
rest
set
those

5. How much?
anything
bit
enough
everything
except
full
half
nothing
part
piece
quite
really
such

third
whole
without

6. How old?
age
old
young

7. How valuable?
cost
dollars
money
treasure

8. What kind?
broken
deep
different
hard
main
real
same
sharp
soft
straight
strong
wide

Location

1. Buildings
bank
cabin
castle
hospital
hut
shed
shop
station

2. Parts of a building
attic
cellar
door
floor
gate
roof
stairs
upstairs
wall
window
* *
bedroom
hall
kitchen
lounge

3. Places
airport
city
country
farm
field
garden
market
paddock
street
town
track
village

4. Where?
aboard
across
against
base
behind
beside
bottom
corner
everywhere
front
high
inside
middle
outside
somewhere
together
top
towards
upon
* *
course
east
north
south
west

Nature

1. Animals
bird
cat
crocodile
dinosaur
fish
hare
horse
lion
mouse
pig
shark
sheep
squid
whale
wolf
* *
cage
feed
fly
hay
pet
trap

2. Body parts
blood
bone
ear
eyes
face
feet
foot
hair
hand
leg
mouth
neck
nose
stomach
tail
teeth
* *
sight

3. Colours
black
blue
brown
gold
green
orange
pink
red
white
yellow
* *
bright
dark

4. Matter
earth
mud
rock
sand
* *
burnt
fire
smoke

5. Places
beach
cave
ground
hill
hole
island
land
mountain

6. Plants
bush
flower
forest
grass
leaves

7. Sounds
bang
bell
boom
crackers
crash
fireworks
loud
noise
quiet
ring
* *
hear
laughed
screamed
shouted
yelled

8. Space
moon
planet
sky
sun
world

9. Water
flood
ice
lake
pool
river
snow
stream
* *
drip

10. Weather
blow
cold
fine
hot
rain
storm
sunny
warm
wet
wind

Common Objects

1. Containers
bag
bottle
box
case
cup
sack

2. Clothes

hat
jersey
pants
shirt
socks
togs
T-shirt
* *
shoes

3. Food

bread
cake
cream
drink
egg
meat
milk
* *
cook

4. House contents

bed
carpet
chair
clock
curtain
dishes
oven
picture
radio
table
TV

5. Materials

board
clothes
paper
rope
stick
wood

People

1. Family

aunt
brother
cousin
dad
granddad
grandfather
grandma
grandmother
grandpa
husband
mum
parents
sister
uncle
wife
* *
married

2. Others

anyone
baby
everybody
everyone
herself
himself
lady
myself
person
someone
woman
* *
alien
army
baby-sitter
captain
clown
crew
dwarf
elf
ghost
God
guard
king
leader
monster
police
warrior
witch

Activities

1. Daily events

asleep
breakfast
dinner
dream
dress
hungry
job
lunch
lying
news
sleep
tea
tired
wake
wash

2. Feelings

care
cry
enjoy
feel
hate
hope
love
need
please
wish

3. Fighting

cannon
fight
gun
kill
shoot
war

4. Games

bat
catch
match
net
race
rugby
softball
team
tennis
throw
win

5. Leisure
arcade
adventure
camp
circus
club
film
fun
music
park
party
picnic
riding
running
swim
tent
toy
trip

6. Movements
began
climb
close
crept
cross
dropped
fall
flapping
followed
grow
hopped
jump
knock
move
passed
pull
rushed
shake
slide
sit
stand
start
turn
wandered
*   *
cause

7. Not moving
die
finish
stay
stop
wait

8. Other actions
able
allowed
arrived
became
bring
build
buy
carried
cut
display
happen
hide
hit
hold
hurt
keep
lead
leave
meet
miss
packed
pick
ripped
sent
show
smashed
sold
tied
try
use
visit
watch

9. School
class
forget
learn
letter
mark
maths
prize
remember
story
teacher
test
write

10. Talking
ask
call
replied
talk
voice
*   *
hello
oh

11. Thinking
believe
decided
idea
mean
mind
plan
seemed
true
wrong

12. Transport
aeroplane
bike
boat
bus
car
jeep
plane
ship
spaceship
train
truck
*   *
drive
engine
machine
motor
power
ride
rocket

Descriptions

1. Pleasant
beautiful
clean
enjoyed
excited
favourite
friendly
funny
glad
happy
interesting
lovely
lucky
neat
nice
own
pretty
quietly
safe
sure

2. Unpleasant
angry
bad
dangerous
dirty
mad
poor
sad
scared
sick
terrible
ugly

3. Unusual
disappeared
haunted
invisible
lost
strange
weird
*   *
surprise

Shortened Words
can't
couldn't
didn't
doesn't
don't
haven't
he's
I'd
I'll
I'm
it's
I've
let's
that's
they're
there's
wasn't
what's
where's
who's
won't
wouldn't

Commonly Misspelt Words

The 55 words in this section are among the most difficult to spell correctly. As they are often used in writing, it is important that you learn to spell each one.

allowed	disappeared	holidays	stopped
awhile	doesn't	hopped	straight
believe	dollars	hospital	they're
breakfast	don't	instead	threw
brought	everybody	lightning	tomorrow
cannon	everyday	luckily	video
can't	everywhere	nearly	wasn't
caught	excited	police	watch
centre	favourite	present	weren't
chocolate	field	probably	we're
clothes	friends	quiet	whole
couldn't	front	scared	won't
didn't	grabbed	second	you're
different	having	someone	

Hints
on Spelling other words

Here are some hints on how to spell other words by changing the final letter(s) of some words in *Spell-Write*.

1. **'s'** may be added to some words **without changing** other letters.

Examples   crumb ⟶ crumb**s**   win ⟶ win**s**

dance ⟶ dance**s**   animal ⟶ animal**s**

Words that may have **'s'** added without changing other letters often end in: 'a', 'b', 'c', 'd', 'e', 'h', 'k', 'l', 'm', 'n', 'p', 'r', 't', 'w', 'y'.

2. **'r'** may be added to some words **without changing** other letters.

Examples   drive ⟶ drive**r**   grade ⟶ grade**r**

pipe ⟶ pipe**r**

Words that may have **'r'** added without changing other letters usually end in 'e'.

3. **'d'** may be added to some words **without changing** other letters.

Examples   dance ⟶ dance**d**   raise ⟶ raise**d**

use ⟶ use**d**   space ⟶ space**d**

Words that may have **'d'** added without changing other letters usually also end in 'e'.

4. **'ed'** may be added to some words **without changing** other letters.

Examples   add ⟶ add**ed**   wait ⟶ wait**ed**

seem ⟶ seem**ed**   join ⟶ join**ed**

Words that may have **'ed'** added without changing other letters often end in: 'b', 'd', 'k', 'l', 'm', 'n', 'p', 'r', 't', 'w'.

5. **'es'** may be added to some words **without changing** other letters.

Examples   branch → branch**es**   potato → potato**es**

vanish → vanish**es**   mix → mix**es**

Words that may have **'es'** added without changing other letters often end in: 'ch', 'o', 'ss', 'sh', 'to', 'x'.

6. **'ing'** may be added to some words **without changing** other letters.

Examples   find → find**ing**   shout → shout**ing**

jump → jump**ing**   spill → spill**ing**

Words that may have **'ing'** added without changing other letters often end in: 'b', 'd', 'f', 'h', 'k', 'l', 'm', 'n', 'o', 'p', 'r', 't', 'w', 'x', 'y'.

7. **'ing'** may be added to some words after **doubling** the last letter.

Examples   sit → sitt**ing**   stop → stopp**ing**

dig → digg**ing**   begin → beginn**ing**

Final letters that are doubled before **'ing'** is added, often include: 'bb', 'gg', 'll', 'mm', 'nn', 'pp', 'rr', 'tt'.

8. **'ing'** may be added after **dropping** the final e.

Examples   remov~~e~~ → remov**ing**   hop~~e~~ → hop**ing**

smil~~e~~ → smil**ing**   com~~e~~ → com**ing**

After the final 'e' has been dropped, the letter before **'ing'** is added is often: 'c', 'g', 'k', 'l', 'm', 'n', 'p', 'r', 's', 't', 'u', 'v', 'z'.

Try out these hints and find words in *Spell-Write* that do and do not fit each one. This is a way of helping you to improve your spelling.